Published by Canon Press
P.O. Box 8729, Moscow, Idaho 83843
800.488.2034 | www.canonpress.com

Toby Sumpter, *Worldview Guide for The Adventures of Tom Sawyer*
Copyright ©2018 by Toby J. Sumpter.
Cited page numbers come from the Canon Classics edition (2017), www.
canonpress.com/books/canon-classics.

Cover design by James Engerbretson
Cover illustration by Forrest Dickison
Interior design by Valerie Anne Bost and James Engerbretson

Printed in the United States of America.

Library of Congress Cataloging-in-Publication Data
Sumpter, Toby, author.
The adventures of Tom Sawyer worldview guide / Toby Sumpter.
Moscow, Idaho : Canon Press, [2018]
LCCN 2019011349 | ISBN 9781947644229 (paperback : alk. paper)
LCSH: Twain, Mark, 1835-1910. Adventures of Tom Sawyer.
Classification: LCC PS1306 .S86 2018 | DDC 813/.4--dc23
LC record available at https://lccn.loc.gov/2019011349

A free end-of-book test and answer key are available for download at
www.canonpress.com/ClassicsQuizzes

18 19 20 21 22 23   9 8 7 6 5 4 3

WORLDVIEW GUIDE

THE ADVENTURES OF TOM SAWYER

Toby J. Sumpter

canonpress
Moscow, Idaho

CONTENTS

INTRODUCTION

Ah, *childhood*. Boys. Long summer days, barefoot, fishing, swimming, laughter, pocket knives, dirty hands, dirty faces, sweaty brows, trouble, *joy*. *The Adventures of Tom Sawyer* is an unmistakable celebration of youth and in particular *boyhood*. At the same time, it's an extended commentary on adulthood, grownups, society, and culture. And that commentary largely consists of a long, exaggerated eye-roll. Welcome to one of the great American stories. Welcome to the wit and the wonder of one of America's greatest writers.

THE WORLD AROUND

The Adventures of Tom Sawyer appeared at the end 1876, the same year the Ottoman Empire ended and a severe famine broke out in China, eventually claiming some 30 million lives and becoming the 5th worst famine in recorded history. The Franco-Prussian War had kicked off the decade, out of which the German Empire began to rise under the leadership of Otto von Bismark. Queen Victoria reigned in England, continuing to grow the British Empire around the world.

In America, Alexander Graham Bell applied for the first telephone patent, and having received it, made the first phone call with the words, "Mr. Watson, come here, I want to see you." By the end of the decade, Thomas Edison had invented the phonograph and the light bulb.

While Reconstruction came to an end in the South after the election of Rutherford B. Hayes—one of the most contested presidential elections in American history—the

American Indian Wars grew in intensity in the West, including the Battle of Little Bighorn, in which 300 soldiers under the command of Lieutenant Colonel Custer were killed by 5,000 Indians led by Sitting Bull and Crazy Horse.

The Transcontinental Express brought the first passengers to San Francisco, 83 hours and 39 minutes after leaving New York City. And many of the famous and infamous lawmen and outlaws roamed the wild west: Wyatt Erp began work as law enforcement in Dodge City, Kansas, while Wild Bill Hickok, Jesse James, Calamity Jane, and countless others, held up stagecoaches, robbed banks, rustled cattle, and rode into at least a few sunsets.

The same year *Tom Sawyer* appeared, America celebrated its centennial birthday with, among other things, the first official World's Fair in Philadelphia, Pennsylvania.

ABOUT THE AUTHOR

Mark Twain was born Samuel Langhorne Clemens on November 30, 1835, shortly after the appearance of Halley's Comet.

Clemens grew up Hannibal, Missouri, a bustling port town on the Mississippi River, leaving school after fifth grade and becoming an apprentice printer at the *Hannibal Courier*. At 21, he began learning how to pilot a steamboat on the Mississippi, but his steamboat career ended with the outbreak of the Civil War in 1861. While Clemens briefly enlisted with the Confederate Army, his volunteer unit disbanded after only two weeks, so he hopped onto a stagecoach heading out West to seek his fortune in the gold rush. After a year without success, Clemens went to work as a reporter for the *Virginia City Territorial Enterprise* in Virginia City, Nevada.

It was while writing news stories, editorials, and other humorous sketches that he donned the pen name "Mark

Twain," which is steamboat slang for two fathoms deep or twelve feet of water—the safe depth for a steamboat. Later, he moved to San Francisco, and in 1865, he achieved his first literary success when "The Celebrated Jumping Frog of Calaveras County" was published. He married Olivia Langdon in February 1870, and they had four children together, taking up residence in Hartford, Connecticut, next door to Harriet Beecher Stowe. In 1909, Thomas Edison visited Twain and took what is thought to be the only existing film footage of him.

In the same year, Twain predicted that he would die when Halley's comet came back by the following year: "The Almighty has said, no doubt: 'Now here are these two unaccountable freaks; they came in together, they must go out together.'" And on April 21, 1910, the day after the comet's closest approach to earth, Twain died of a heart attack.

WHAT OTHER NOTABLES SAID

"An average American loves his family. If he has any love left over for some other person, he generally selects Mark Twain."
~Thomas Edison

"To my mind Mark Twain was beyond question the largest man of his time, both in direct outcome of his work and more important still, if possible, in his indirect influence as a protesting force in an age of iron philistinism."
~Rudyard Kipling

"He talked delightfully, audaciously, brilliantly... his talk fragrant with tobacco and flamboyant with profanity. He seemed to have absorbed all America into himself."
~Helen Keller

William Faulkner called Twain, "the father of American literature."

When Twain died, President William Howard Taft said, "Mark Twain gave pleasure—real intellectual enjoyment—to millions, and his works will continue to give such pleasure to millions yet to come…. His humor was American, but he was nearly as much appreciated by Englishmen and people of other countries as by his own countrymen. He has made an enduring part of American literature."

CHARACTERS, SETTING AND PLOT SUMMARY

- Thomas "Tom" Sawyer: The main character and hero of the story. Tom is about 12 years old and loves playing Robin Hood and Pirates with his friends, cutting school, avoiding work, and showing off
- Aunt Polly: Tom lives with his Aunt Polly, sister of Tom and Sid's deceased mother. She is a disciplinarian and fussy, but at heart a truly caring character
- Sidney "Sid": Tom's half-brother who also lives with Aunt Polly and enjoys getting Tom into trouble
- Mary: Tom Sawyer's cousin, Aunt Polly's daughter
- Huckleberry Finn: Tom's best friend, son of the town drunk, free-roaming boy

- Joe Harper: Tom's other best friend, joins Tom and Huck when they run away to Jackson's Island
- Becky Thatcher: The daughter of the new judge in town, Judge Thatcher, and Tom's crush.
- Doctor Robinson: Murdered by Injun Joe during an attempted grave robbery.
- Injun Joe: Main antagonist in the story, murdered Dr. Robinson for a petty grievance, and aims to harm others
- Muff Potter: A friendly town drunk who is framed by Injun Joe for the murder of Dr. Robinson
- Widow Douglas: Cares for Huck when he gets sick, widow of the deceased Judge Douglas. Huck hears Injun Joe plotting to harm her in revenge for his husband's treatment of him.
- Mr. Dobbins: The short-tempered schoolmaster in St. Petersburg, MO.

The Adventures of Tom Sawyer centers on Tom who lives in St. Petersburg, Missouri, a port town along the Mississippi River, with his long-suffering and insufferable Aunt Polly, and Sid and Mary. The time period is likely sometime before the Civil War. He spends most of his time with his best friends Huckleberry Finn and Joe Harper, when he isn't trying to impress or win the love of Becky Thatcher.

When Huckleberry tells Tom that heaving a dead cat at spirits in a graveyard after a recent burial is a way to get rid of warts, they decide to give it a try and accidentally witness the murder of Doctor Robinson by Injun Joe who frames Muff Potter. For fear of Injun Joe, Tom, Huck, and Joe run away to Jackson's Island in the middle of the Mississippi river, and are eventually given up for dead. But after Muff Potter is narrowly exonerated, Injun Joe escapes prosecution, and the adventures continue in abandoned shacks and dark caves, weaving boyish games, fabulous superstitions, midnight escapades, and buried treasure into a timeless adventure.

WORLDVIEW ANALYSIS

Mark Twain's classic work is a big grin and a wink and a nod at the glory of childhood, and *boys* in particular. But this celebration of boyhood isn't in a vacuum; there is a clear target to Twain's lampooning: a certain bureaucratic bumbling, a stuffy legalism, a fussy Pharisaism, the unmistakable cranky old man syndrome. From Aunt Polly's medicinal quackery and emotional superciliousness to the mind-numbing preacher to the show dog Sunday School teacher, the hypocrisies are thick and stifling. And Twain invites us to cheer when Tom thwarts their designs with his wit and folly, accidental or intended.

In one of the early and most legendary scenes, Tom outwits his Aunt Polly's designs to keep him occupied all day with the laborious assignment of white-washing a fence, and he succeeds in this by engendering the envy of all the neighborhood children and getting them to pay *him* for a chance to white-wash the fence. Twain writes:

> And when the middle of the afternoon came, from
> being a poor poverty-stricken boy in the morning,
> Tom was literally rolling in wealth. He had besides
> the things before mentioned, twelve marbles, part
> of a jews-harp, a piece of blue bottle-glass to look
> through, a spool cannon, a key that wouldn't unlock
> anything, a fragment of chalk, a glass stopper of
> a decanter, a tin soldier, a couple of tadpoles, six
> fire-crackers, a kitten with only one eye, a brass
> door-knob, a dog-collar –but no dog—the handle
> of a knife, four pieces of orange peel, and a dilap-
> idated old window sash…. Tom said to himself it
> was not such a hollow world, after all. He had dis-
> covered a great law of human action, without know-
> ing it—namely, that in order to make a man or a
> boy covet a thing, it is only necessary to make the
> thing difficult to attain…. Work consists of whatev-
> er a body is obliged to do, and that Play consists of
> whatever a body is not obliged to do. (13-14)[1]

Here, Twain captures with characteristic wit a deep pleasure in the curiosities and absurdities and obsessions of boyhood alongside the slothful tendencies of human nature.

In another scene, having "won" a number of Bible memory tickets as a result of trading the wealth he had acquired in the fence white-washing business, Tom is introduced to the new judge in town as the winner of a brand new Bible. With the whole church looking on and the Sunday School teacher trying to make a good impression on the new judge, the judge speaks to Tom:

---

1. All quotes are taken from the Canon Classics edition (2016), .

"That's a good boy. Fine boy. Fine, manly little fellow. Two thousand verses is a great many—very, very great many. And you never can be sorry for the trouble you took to learn them; for knowledge is worth more than anything there is in the world; it's what makes great men and good men; you'll be a great man and a good man yourself, some day, Thomas, and then you'll look back and say, It's all owing to the precious Sunday-school privileges of my boyhood…. And now you wouldn't mind telling me and this lady some the things you've learned— no, I know you wouldn't—for we are proud of little boys that learn. Now, no doubt you know the names of the twelve disciples. Won't you tell us the names of the first two that were appointed?"

Tom was tugging at the button-hole and looking sheepish. He blushed, now, and his eyes fell. Mr. Walters' heart sank within him. He said to himself, it is not possible that the boy can answer the simplest question—why did the Judge ask him? Yet he felt obliged to speak up and say:

"Answer the gentleman, Thomas—don't be afraid."

Tom still hung fire.

"Now I know you'll tell me," said the lady. "The names of the first two disciples were—"

"David and Goliath!"

> Let us draw the curtain of charity over the rest of
> the scene. (31)

So what is a Christian to make of *Tom Sawyer*? The Bible unmistakably celebrates childhood too. Adam and Eve were like children in the Garden of Eden. The promise of the gospel to Adam and Eve after the Fall was to come through their "seed," a *child* would be born, and that promise was reiterated to Abraham, Isaac, and Jacob. Children figure prominently in many of the biblical stories: from the barrenness of Sarah and the birth of Isaac to the deception of the Hebrew midwives and the birth Moses. The Psalms celebrate children as the blessing of God: they are like arrows in the hand of a warrior, olive plants around the table (Ps. 127, 128). Out of the mouths of babies and infants, God ordains strength (Ps. 8). Isaiah foretold the coming of a great child king: "For to us a child is born, to us a son is given…," a child that would lead leopards and young goats and lions and calves to graze peacefully together (Is. 9:6, 11:6-7).

And Jesus famously welcomed children, designating them as model citizens of the Kingdom (Mt. 19:14). Unless you are converted and become like children, you cannot enter the Kingdom. Jesus made the same point with Nicodemus: Unless you are born again, you cannot enter the Kingdom (Jn. 3:3). You must become a child somehow by the Spirit. Even "eternal life" seems to be related to all of this. Eternal life is unending life—or we might say eternal life is eternal *youth*. If you'll never die, then you can't really be said to grow *old*. If there is no end in sight, then you're never any closer to the end. If you have eternal life, you might be adding days to your story but from the vantage of eternity, you're still just as *young*.

Arguably, much of the life of Jesus is taken up with a Tom Sawyer-like ministry in Israel. When he was twelve, he began debating with the teachers of the Law in Jerusalem and gave his parents the slip after the feast (Lk. 2:42-50). The Pharisees and Priests and Scribes really are a bunch of Aunt Pollys and Sunday School superintendents. And Jesus walked through their world defying all their superstitions and legalisms and taboos: plucking heads of grain, healing on the Sabbath, eating and drinking with sinners, walking on water, not washing for dinner, pushing over the tables in the temple, staying out all night, calling names, and ultimately coming back from the dead and bursting out of a guarded tomb alive forever. And all of this fits with the mission of God to destroy sin and death and renew the human race. When Adam sinned and brought death into the world, the human race began to grow old. We all began to "grow up" in that terribly stuffy and cranky sense. This is what sin and death does to all of us. It steals our joy, and it makes us insufferable grownups. Jesus came to make us young again. He came to give us eternal life, eternal *youth* through the power of His eternally youthful Spirit.

And yet, this isn't all there is to say. The youthfulness of Christ is not a call to eternal immaturity. There is a kind of childishness that never learns, never grows, never increases in wisdom. That kind of childishness is called *folly*. And the Bible says that folly must be driven out of the hearts of children (Prov. 22:15). Likewise, Jesus calls His disciples to become wise as serpents, innocent as doves—to be like the wise man who builds his house on the rock of obedience to God's word. While Christians are to long for the milk of the word like newborn babies, they are also to grow up and eat solid food, the meat of doctrinal wisdom (1 Cor. 3:2; 1 Pet. 2:2). "But solid food is for the mature, for those who have their powers of discernment trained by constant practice to distinguish good from evil" (Heb. 5:11-14). Constant practice takes time, learning lessons, a good memory, developing skills, and all of that is what the Bible calls "maturity."

So which is it? Are we supposed to be children or adults in Christ? Youthful or mature? Well, the biblical answer seems to be "yes." The kind of childishness we are called to doesn't resent learning, progress, or wisdom. The call of Christ is to grow up into the sort of mature wisdom and youthful liveliness He possesses. God is innocent, creative, jovial, energetic, not a crank, not a grump, not a whiner. But God is also terribly wise, absolutely just, patient, gracious, and He is not impulsive, not easily distracted, not naïve. In other words, there are characteristics of youth and maturity that reflect the goodness and glory of God that we are called to emulate by the power of God's Holy Spirit.

So let's push this out into the corners: Do you prefer the city or the country? A balcony in a high rise overlooking a cityscape of lights and sounds and people or a rustic porch on a rural hillside with snowcapped mountains shooting up in the distance? Are you agrarian or metropolitan?

Shift the question slightly: Do you prefer a hospital in a big city or grandma's herbal tea remedy? Would you prefer leeches for your fever or Tylenol? A horse drawn carriage or a Ford pickup? Porridge every night of the week or Chinese on Monday, Mexican on Tuesday, Italian on Wednesday…? Electricity or no electricity? Forced air heat and air conditioning or just windows and a fireplace? Indoor plumbing or an outhouse? Internet or no internet?

Hopefully you get the point. Of course not all of these trade offs are created equal. Many answers would have to be: "it depends." Proverbs says, "Better is a dinner of herbs where love is than a fattened ox and hatred with it" (Prov. 15:17). Sometimes modern medicine can really mess things up (e.g. abortion, transgender surgeries, etc.), but on the whole I'd probably rather take my chances in a modern hospital than with a field doctor who has whiskey and a hacksaw as his primary tools of healing. Grandma's herbal tea might be good for the common cold, but I'm very grateful for x-rays and ultrasounds and MRIs and antibiotics. The internet can be used to do many evil things, but it is also being used to spread the gospel around the globe.

What we're talking about is the relative goods of progress, tradition, and technology. The mechanisms where these goods are stored and passed on are in the cultures of families, churches, schools, cities, and nations. On the whole, Tom Sawyer doesn't have much use for church or school—and family is perhaps a well meaning but rather stifling structure. But the Bible teaches that God has given good things to our families and cultures in the past that we should be slow and reluctant to give up. The Bible says that we should not remove the ancient landmark (Prov. 22:28). It says to honor your father and mother (Ex. 20:12). The same Jesus who overturned tables in the temple said He came to *build* His Church in this world. This means that in general we should expect that God has been storing up glory for us through these institutions that have come before us. We need families, schools, and churches to hand down those goods from the past, the wisdom of the past, so that we can be good stewards with that wealth (e.g. information, technology) in the present and future.

However, there can also be an idolization of the past. People sometimes romanticize the past: back in the good old days, they say, and everything in the present is ugly and evil and descending into the depths of depravity. And of course sometimes that's true. But there can also be an idolization and romanticizing of the present and future. Twain seems to verge on that romanticizing—lifting up Tom's carefree present-tense focus as a wonderful ideal—and yet for all the joy of Tom's boyishness, a civilization of Tom Sawyers would never build hospitals, invent air-planes, or program computers. You can often map these opposing tendencies to generations: younger people often resent the ways of their parents and grandparents, and older folks can resent the ways of youth.

But God intended for the strengths and glories of old age and youth to be friends, not adversaries. Technology is the accumulation of man hours spent creating, discovering, building, thinking, discussing, planning, experimenting, exploring, and learning. Technology is humanity *growing up*. The human race was given this task in the beginning when God created the heavens and the earth and told Adam and Eve to be fruitful and multiply, to make more people and fill the world and make it glorious. This necessarily implies *maturity*, learning, studying, improving, building upon yesterday, last year, last century. But the energy and audacity and creativity required to keep trying new things, to re-organize, to re-think, to look somewhere new or at a problem or need from a new angle implies *youthfulness*. We need both, and the work of the gospel, seen from one angle, is precisely this. Our Old Testament ends with this promise for the New Covenant in Jesus: "Behold, I will send you Elijah the prophet before the great and awesome day of the LORD comes. And he will turn the hearts of the fathers to their children and the hearts of children to their fathers…" (Mal. 4:5-6).

The promise of the gospel is not merely that families will not squabble so much. No, the promise is so much grander than that. The promise of the gospel is about blessing for all the families of the earth. It's about carrying out what Adam and Eve were originally commissioned to do, to finish what sin and death have interrupted. So Jesus has come to reconcile us to God by dying for our sin, and by rising to new life in order to make all things new. This new creation includes reconciliation of peoples, of families, of nations, of ethnicities, and all of this entails the restoration of God's blessing on the sciences and technology and arts and industries and so on.

Clearly, Mark Twain's *Tom Sawyer* is a fun and lighthearted poke at adulthood gone to seed. At points, Twain may verge on a certain romanticism of boyhood. Of course, God loves boys—He invented them. Boys have a unique and fascinating glory, but they are also, not to put too fine a point on it, part of the problem with this fallen world. In other words, boys are *sinful.* Mark Twain does seem to have some knowledge of this when he recognizes the foibles and follies of the boys. Tom and Huck heaving a dead cat at spirits in a graveyard at midnight is just as superstitious as any of Aunt Polly's schemes. But for all the welcome delight in boyhood, it isn't clear that Twain is actually presenting a solution. A world run by boys would be no more delightful than a world run by Aunt Pollys or vapid preachers. Speaking of those problems, Tom and Becky's "romance" while amusing at points is hardly an ideal. Turns out when that kind of emotional compulsiveness drives what we consider romance, you end up with a modern world like the one we live in with one-night stands and out of wedlock pregnancy and abortion on demand—nothing innocent or cute about it. Some sins seem cute when they're little but they grow up to be nasty, destructive demons.

Nevertheless, to the extent that Tom Sawyer is offered as a *corrective* to cranky traditionalism, he should be welcomed with a cheer. There are plenty of places in our world that need a joyful, vigorous, childlike disruption. In the old fable of the Emperor's New Clothes, it was a little boy who pointed out that the emperor was *naked*. In a world that pretends that two men or two women can be married, or that a man who was born as a biological male can do anything to change himself into a woman is a world where we are proclaiming *impossibilities* with a serious grownup voice. The emperor is not wearing clothes at all. He's naked. We need piles of Christians to take a note from Tom Sawyer's playbook. You need to play hookie from what the respectable worldly Pharisees have cooked up. No, we won't be attending your diversity training awareness classes. No, we won't play by your rules. And when they come to scold you or fine you (or worse), just imagine them as a bunch of Aunt Pollys and slip out your window in the night. The world our Father made is far more interesting than all their silly superstitions. It really is hard to take all those "no smoking" and "gluten free" signs seriously when abortion and sodomy run rampant in our land. So find yourself a church on some Jackson's Island—one that takes Jesus seriously and sees discipleship as something like playing Robin Hood for real. But don't stop there. Put down roots: marry your Becky Thatcher and raise children together, build schools, plant churches, and invest them with the wisdom of Jesus our Child King, the One who went down into the darkest cave of death and came out alive forever—the One who has secured eternal youth for us.

QUOTABLES

1. "The old lady pulled her spectacles down and looked over them about the room; then she put them up and looked out under them. She seldom or never looked through them for so small a thing as a boy; they were her state pair, the pride of her heart, and were built for 'style,' not service—she could have seen through a pair of stove-lids just as well."
    ~Narrator, p. 1

2. "She was one of those people who are infatuated with patent medicines and all new-fangled methods of producing health or mending it. She was an inveterate experimenter in these things. When something fresh in this line came out she was in a fever, right away, to try it; not on herself, for she was never ailing, but on anybody else that came handy. She was a subscriber for all the "Health" periodicals and phrenological frauds…. She was as simple-hearted and honest as the day was

long, and so she was an easy victim. She gathered her quack periodicals and her quack medicines, and thus armed with death, went about on her pale horse, metaphorically speaking, with 'hell following after.'"
~Narrator, pp. 80-81

3. "The choir always tittered and whispered all through service. There was once a church choir that was not ill-bred, but I have forgotten where it was, now. It was a great many years ago, and I can scarcely remember anything about it, but I think it was in some foreign country."
    ~Narrator, p. 33

4. "Often, the less there is to justify a traditional custom, the harder it is to get rid of it."
    ~Narrator, pp. 33-34

5. "Tom was a glittering hero once more—the pet of the old, the envy of the young.... There were some that believed he would be President, yet, if he escaped hanging."
    ~Narrator, p. 152

21 SIGNIFICANT QUESTIONS AND ANSWERS

1. What does Chapter 1 tell you about the kind of boy Tom is?

   Tom is mischievous, clever, brave, skips school, lies, and is regularly in trouble with his aunt.

2. What is Aunt Polly like? Give three examples that demonstrate your description.

   Aunt Polly is well-meaning, superstitious, endearing, and a bit gullible and sentimental. Her attempts at discipline are humorous: looking for Tom when he's hiding in the closet eating jam, questioning Tom when she suspects he's played hookie, her "medicinal" attempts to cure Tom, her response to Tom's return after his disappearance, her punishment of Tom after he fed the cat the pain-killer, etc.

3.   What is church like in St. Petersburg, MO?

>   Sunday School is a bit of a charade of showing kids
>   off for their memory work. Sunday service is dry,
>   boring, and the preacher apparently spends most of
>   his time whittling down the elect to a number so
>   small it seemed hardly worth saving.

4.   Describe Tom's play with Huck and Joe. List some of
     their games.

>   There's a good deal of talk about various supersti-
>   tious theories of curing warts and such. They play
>   Robin Hood in Sherwood Forest, Pirates (Black
>   Avenger of the Spanish Main), after a revival
>   sweeps through town they form the Cadets of
>   Temperance, and at the end of the book, they are
>   planning to form a Gang of Robbers.

5.   Describe the storm on the island. What significance
     may those details give to the larger themes in the story?

>   The storm is at night and comes on slowly from
>   the distance, lightning glowing in the distance,
>   then a quiet breath of wind, then a bright flash
>   and a deep peal of thunder, then a great wind and
>   heavy rain that eventually tears away the old ship
>   mast that served as their tent. The boys take refuge
>   under a great oak near the riverbank, with thunder
>   rumbling and lightening flashing and trees crashing
>   down every few minutes. Seems likely that the
>   storm represents some of the wildness and beauty
>   of nature. It is dangerous, but it is also sublime,

awe-inspiring. The island adventures along with the storm represent Twain's romanticism of nature.

6. How do the townsfolk respond when Tom, Huck, and Joe reappear alive at their own funeral?

> Everyone lavishes them with hugs and kisses and thanksgivings. The minister led the congregation in singing "Praise God from whom all blessings flow," and the congregation thought the singing was so good they'd almost be willing to have it happen all over again just to hear it sung that well again.

7. What do Chapters 19 and 20 tell you about the kind of boy Tom is?

> Despite all of Tom's mischief, he really does mean well. In Chapter 19, he demonstrates this by explaining that his lie about his dream of seeing Aunt Polly was true, that he had kissed her in her sleep, and decided not to leave the piece of bark telling her he'd gone pirating. She finds the piece of bark in his jacket, confirming the truth of his story. In Chapter 20, we see Tom take the blame for the spilled ink in his spelling book (another boy had done it and Becky Thatcher knew about it). He also takes the blame for Becky Thatcher when she accidentally ripped a page from the schoolmaster's special book he kept under lock and key.

8. Describe some of the highlights of "Examination Day" at the school.

> The exercises included some poetry recitations. Tom recited half of his memory work before getting stage fright and eventually giving up. A great many girls gave declamations full of nursed melancholy, wasteful gushes of fine language, overused words and phrases, and many moralistic sermons at the end of each one. Finally, when the schoolmaster attempted to lead a geography demonstration, a cat was let down from the ceiling that grabbed his wig off his head, revealing a shiny, painted bald pate. And that ended the meeting.

9. What happens at Muff Potter's hearing?

> Tom Sawyer is called as a surprise witness, and he testifies to having seen Injun Joe kill the doctor in the graveyard. After this testimony is given, Injun Joe escapes out of a window.

10. Why do the boys go to the haunted house?

> The boys go to the haunted house looking for buried treasure.

11. What do the boys see and overhear at the haunted house?

> The "deaf and dumb" Spaniard and another man show up at the haunted house while Tom and Huck are upstairs. When the "deaf and dumb" Spaniard

begins speaking they realize at once that it's Injun
Joe in disguise. They see that he and the other man
have hidden $650 worth of silver under a floor
board, and they watch as a box full of thousands of
dollars' worth of gold coins is unearthed beneath
their own stash. Tom and Huck hear the plan to
bury the gold under "Number Two—under the
cross." They barely escape discovery when Injun Joe
falls through the rotten stairs trying to come up to
search the attic.

12. What does Huckleberry find out that Injun Joe is planning to do to Widow Douglas? Why?

Huck finds out that Injun Joe is planning to slit her
nostrils and notch her ears as revenge for the time
when her (now deceased) husband horsewhipped
him in front of the jail.

13. How does it come out to the Welshman who the "deaf
and dumb Spaniard" is? Who is it?

After Huck went to the Welshman's house for help
to protect the Widow Douglas, the old Welshman
later questioned him about how he came to be
following the two men who were plotting against
Widow Douglas. In the course of the questioning it
came out that the "deaf and dumb" Spaniard could
talk and Huck eventually confessed that it was
Injun Joe.

14. When do Tom and Becky turn up missing?

> After church on Sunday morning, when Mrs.
> Thatcher asked Mrs. Harper if Becky would sleep
> all day, assuming she had stayed with her overnight
> as Becky had said she planned to do. Likewise,
> Aunt Polly assumed Tom had stayed with someone
> else overnight. At that point, no one recalls seeing
> Tom and Becky on the ferryboat, and someone
> eventually concludes they were left in the caves.

15. How did Tom and Becky get lost in the caves?

> Tom and Becky had wandered a good way when
> they were chased by bats through a number of
> chambers and passages. Finally, when they are rid of
> the bats and try to go back, they cannot find their
> way.

16. Who does Tom see in the caves?

> While Tom is trying to explore and find a way out
> of the caves, he suddenly comes upon Injun Joe.

17. How did Tom and Becky finally find their way out?

> Tom tied kite-line to a projection in the rock and
> used that to explore the side caves and eventually
> he saw a tiny speck of light that turned out to be a
> hidden entrance to the caves right next to the river.

18. Why does Tom turn "white as a sheet" when the judge tells him the cave has been locked up securely to keep folks from getting lost in it again? What do they find when they go down and open the cave back up?

> Tom turns white as a sheet because he knows Injun Joe was in the cave. They find Injun Joe dead right inside the door.

19. What does Tom tell Huck is back in the caves? Is he right?

> Tom tells Huck that he's pretty sure the treasure is buried back in the caves, and sure enough it is.

20. When Huck turns up missing from Widow Douglas's care, what does he tell Tom about being rich?

> Huck tells Tom, "Being rich ain't what its' cracked up to be. It's just worry and worry, and sweat and sweat, and a-wishing you was dead all the time" (223)

21. How does Tom convince Huck to come back to the Widow's house?

> Tom tells Huck that he's planning to start a band of robbers, but he won't be able to let Huck in if he doesn't stay with the Widow Douglas because robbers are "more high-toned than what a pirate is... they're awful high up in the nobility—dukes and such." (223)

FURTHER DISCUSSION
AND REVIEW

Master what you have read by reviewing and integrating the different elements of this classic.

SETTING AND CHARACTERS
Be able to compare and contrast the personalities (including strengths, weaknesses, and mannerisms) of each character. Which characters change over the course of the novel? Which do not?

PLOT
Be able to describe the beginning, middle, and end of the book along with specific details that move the plot forward and make it compelling. This includes the success or downfall (or both) of each character.

CONFLICT

Go through the character list and describe the tension between any and all main characters. Then, think about whether any characters have internal conflict (in their own minds). Is there any overt conflict (fighting), or conflict with impersonal forces?

THEME STATEMENTS

Be able to describe what this classic is telling us about the world. Is the message true? What truth can we take from the plot, characters, conflict, and themes (even if the author didn't believe that truth)? Do any objects take on added meaning because of repetition or their place in the story (i.e., do any objects become symbols)? How does the author use perspective, tone, and irony to tell the truth?

- Childhood with its vibrant curiosity and disruptive honesty is something good, though not perfect.
- We need to both appreciate the benefits of time and progress, without being uncritical of it.
- Hypocrisy and corruption in authority is best responded to with a great big guffaw.

Finally, compose your own theme statement about some element, large or small, of this classic. Then, use the Bible and common sense to assess the truth of that theme statement.

TAKING THE CLASSICS QUIZ

Once you have finished the worldview guide, you can prepare for the end-of-book test. Each test will consist of a short-answer section on the book itself and the author, a short-answer section on plot and the narrative, and a long-answer essay section on worldview, conflict, and themes.

Each quiz, along with other helps, can be downloaded for free at www.canonpress.com/ClassicsQuizzes. If you have any questions about the quiz or its answers or the Worldview Guides in general, you can contact Canon Press at service@canonpress.com or 208.892.8074.

ABOUT THE AUTHOR

Toby J. Sumpter is a pastor at Christ Church in Moscow, Idaho, and author of *Blood-Bought World: Jesus, Idols, and the Bible* and the commentary *Job Through New Eyes: A Son for Glory*. He and his wife Jenny live in Moscow, Idaho with their four children. Toby is also a host of the weekly CrossPolitic Show and Podcast.

Made in United States
Orlando, FL
14 October 2024

52627496R00031